C000212946

MORE ODD CORNERS *of the*
G W R
from the Days of Steam

MORE ODD CORNERS *of the* GWR *from the Days of Steam*

KEVIN ROBERTSON

SUTTON PUBLISHING

First published in 2003 by
Sutton Publishing Limited · Phoenix Mill
Thrupp · Stroud · Gloucestershire · GL5 2BU

Copyright © Kevin Robertson, 2003

All rights reserved. No part of this publication may be reproduced, stored in a retrieval system,
or transmitted, in any form, or by any means, electronic, mechanical, photocopying,
recording or otherwise, without the prior permission of the publisher and copyright holder.

Kevin Robertson hereby asserts the moral right to be identified as the author of this work.

British Library Cataloguing in Publication Data
A catalogue record for this book is available from the British Library.

ISBN 0-7509-3219-8

Endpapers: What was once a common local sight: seagoing travellers could disembark on the quayside
in Weymouth, and embark straight away on a train that would carry them to Paddington (or, later,
Waterloo), via the streets of the town.

Frontispiece: Cleaning every nook and cranny, not just the odd corners.

Opposite page: A freight train on the Swansea–Cardiff line, near St Fagans, in June 1949.

Typeset in 10/12 pt Palatino.
Typesetting and origination by
Sutton Publishing Limited.
Printed and bound in England by
J.H. Haynes & Co. Ltd, Sparkford.

Introduction

It was with great pleasure that I received the request to compile a follow-up to the first Great Western Railway volume in the series. Pleasure first of all because the GWR has been and probably always will be a favourite for me, but pleasure also because of the amount of material that continues to be amassed on the company and which now has the chance for exposure.

Unlike the first volume, which arranged material in chapters, for this book I have preferred to present a series of photographs, and I hope these will allow a more extensive spread of topic and a more general appeal. As a longstanding rail enthusiast, I have amassed a large collection of such material. Where I am able to do so definitively, I have given the source of a photograph, and apologise to anyone whose work may have gone so far unacknowledged.

In this volume I have changed the format slightly, from using photographs to illustrate a written theme, to using groups of photographs and allowing them to speak for themselves and through their captions. From correspondence with a number of friends following publication of the first volume, this would seem to be the preferred approach – and who am I to argue with the customer?

I hope that my selection of views will identify both the norm and the unusual. It is tempting in any book such as this to concentrate on the rarities, but to do so is then to ignore the everyday scene, which is itself now only partly visible at such locations as the Severn Valley and West Somerset railways.

Even so, we must be grateful for what has been saved. I heard recently of a photographic archive that had been renamed 'The two-dimensional resource'. In this book, you will find no references to modern management speech or to political correctness. What you will find instead is a glimpse into a past era, through slightly rose-tinted spectacles perhaps – or should that be chocolate and cream?

For those seeking more in-depth information on a specific subject, the number of books on railway subjects should satisfy most interests and a little digging will normally unearth these.

'Nostalgia isn't what it used to be', I have heard people say, and that is the sole reason for an exercise such as this. Sit back and soak up the atmosphere – I only wish I could develop a time machine.

Kevin Robertson

The Great Western Railway as I imagine it to have been – and wish I could have seen it as well. 'Bulldog' No. 3380 *River Yealm* at the head of a Didcot to Reading service, having just left Tilehurst station. (The River Thames is on the right.) What a wonderful selection of vehicles as well, clerestory Thirds, a Dean parcels brake and what appears to be a 'Toplight', second from last. Built in 1903 as No. 3432, the engine was at some point renumbered as seen, and remained in service until March 1938. (*Maurice Earley*)

We commence our tour of different aspects of the GWR with this view of a delightful finish on the paintwork of the reconstructed No. 9 shown here – probably photographed soon after rebuilding in 1884. No. 9 had commenced life as a 4–2–4T tank locomotive under the auspices of the then Swindon supremo, William Dean. However, history records that, due to perhaps understandable instability associated with the 4–2–4T design, it was destined to disgrace itself on its first trip and in consequence was rebuilt in the 2–2–2 form seen here. In later years No. 9 was named *Victoria*, at the same time as having its driving wheel diameter reduced from the 7 ft 8 in shown here to 7 size. Working for some time from Wolverhampton, it survived in service until March 1905. (*Loco Publishing Co.*)

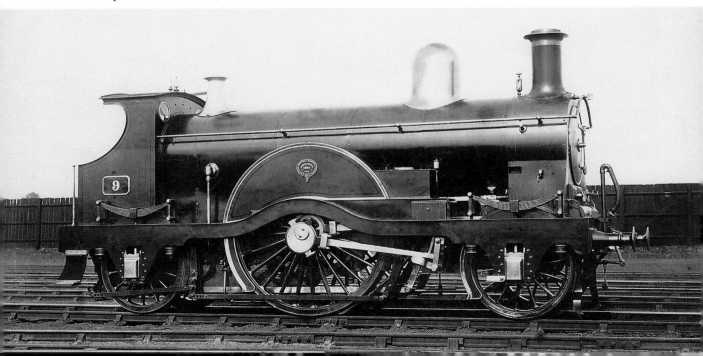

Built to a design dating from the last days of the broad gauge in 1891, the '3031' or 'Achilles' class consisted of no fewer than eighty engines numbered from 3001 to 3080. Eight of these, Nos 3021–8, originally appeared as convertible 2–2–2s, one of which is shown overleaf. No. 3019, built in April 1892, was also a 2–2–2 until May 1894, when it was rebuilt in the form shown, the reason being to increase stability at the front end when running at speed. The result must surely be

aesthetically one of the finest designs ever to run on the GWR, although I appreciate that beauty is very much in the eye of the beholder. Despite her superb external condition, *Rover* would have a short life, surviving only until September 1908, as train weights and required speeds had become too much for the single-driving-wheel design.

No. 3026 was a member of the same class as *Rover* but is depicted here before conversion. Careful study shows a cable linking the locomotive and tender, an early means of emergency communication to the crew when the train was in motion. Like the engine in the previous picture, No. 3026 was also destined for a short life, being withdrawn in 1909, by which time it was named *Tornado*.

The Rhymney Railway contributed 123 locomotives to the GWR at the time of the grouping, including RR No. 31, which had been built by Sharp Stewart as far back as 1872. Of the twenty-one engines in the class, just two were taken over by the GWR. No. 31 was not one of these as it was withdrawn from service in the second half of 1920. (*Loco Publishing Co.*)

The Monmouthshire Railway and Canal Company was amalgamated into the GWR from 1 August 1880 and brought with it some fifty-three steam locomotives. Among these were four 0–6–0T engines, Nos 33–36, built by the Vulcan Foundry in 1865. Rebuilt by the GWR at its Wolverhampton works in 1882 in the form shown here, the engines were renumbered with the addition of '1300' to their previous identities. No. 1335 – after a further rebuild – survived until August 1904, the last of the four in service. (*Loco Publishing Co.*)

Built at Swindon between 1870 and 1881, the 266 engines of the 'Buffalo' class were really the tank equivalent of the then standard goods engines, the 'Dean Goods'. To be found principally in the southern half of the GWR network, the class was equally at home on goods and passenger workings, so much so that their duties included long-distance mineral trains and early morning passenger services. No. 1285 is seen here in what may well be Pembrokeshire with stock in the mixed liveries of chocolate and cream and crimson lake. It was destined to be in service for some fifty-six years, being withdrawn in 1934. (*Loco Publishing Co.*)

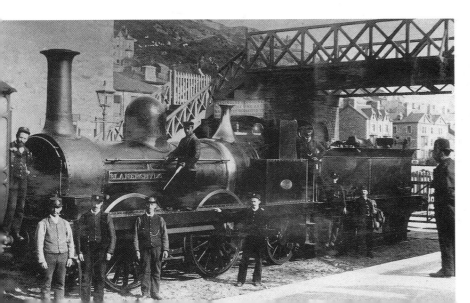

Ordered in 1860 for the Llandilo and Newtown Railway, this delightful little 0–4–2 was one of a class of six similar engines. All were named; this one, No. 7 *Llanerchydol*, is seen here at Aberdovey sometime before June 1891, the date at which it is reported as having its name-plate removed. Withdrawal came in 1898 and none of the class was to pass into GWR ownership. (*Loco Publishing Co.*)

Built in August 1896 at Swindon under the auspices of William Dean, the solitary 4–6–0 design represented by No. 36 was very much the forerunner of the later 'Aberdare' class. Nicknamed 'the Crocodile', the engine was used on heavy freight, working principally through the Severn Tunnel, and in this respect was certainly successful. However, the design was not perpetuated and No. 36 was withdrawn in December 1905, having averaged less than 400 miles each week during its short working life. (*W.J. Reynolds*)

The express service of the turn of the nineteenth century, an unidentified pairing of a 'Metro Tank' piloting what is thought to be a '2201' class 2–4–0 . The train could well be on the Gloucester–Cardiff route, as it is known the 'Metro Tanks' were used for fast workings on this stretch of line. Note that the track has yet to be altered to the later type with conventional sleepers.

No. 644, '633' class 0–6–0T, on another extremely varied train of mixed GWR stock, having just exited the 460-yard Golden Hill tunnel near Pembroke. Such a motley collection of vehicles was by no means uncommon on passenger services, although in later years at least the roof heights tended to be somewhat more consistent.

The forerunners of the later 48xx/14xx type were the 0–4–2Ts of the '517' class, constructed in batches at Wolverhampton between 1868 and 1885. No. 556 seen here appeared in August 1869 and was successively modified and altered over the years – as indeed were most of the class, so ensuring considerable longevity. Indeed No. 556 was destined for a life of no less than sixty-four years, before being finally withdrawn in 1933. The longest lasting of this numerous class was No. 1159, which was in traffic for no less than seventy-one years. (*Millbrook House*)

How better to conclude our glimpse at the earlier days of the GWR than with a view of a train at speed. The 'County' class 4–4–0 depicts the Churchward era while ahead of this as pilot is one of the Dean Singles. The leading vehicle is of non-GWR origin, being an LNWR coach, possibly meaning this was a through working over the 'north and west route' from Shrewsbury.

The specialist doing his stuff – and not a yellow jacket in sight! The photographer is at Kensal Green recording an Up South Wales express, possibly unaware that he too is being recorded for posterity. The wooden box alongside the track is no doubt full of plates ready for the day's filming.

One of George Jackson Churchward's 'Star' class of 1909, which were the mainstay of express passenger workings until the introduction of the 'Castles' in the 1920s. No. 4027 was at this time named *King Henry* but was renamed *The Norwegian Monarch* in July 1927 to avoid confusion with the then new 'King' class engines. Seen waiting to depart from Paddington, the engine would appear to be in original condition and has no doubt received considerable attention from the cleaners. (*Loco Publishing Co.*)

The last remaining example of the 'Star' class, No. 4003, is fortunately preserved. No. 4057 *Princess Elizabeth* was not so lucky and ended up under the cutter's torch. Even so, in their final years, a number of the class were still involved in express workings, as witness No. 4057 on an Up Cheltenham train running through Maidenhead in the early BR period. (*R.F. Dearden*)

All the paraphernalia that goes to make up trackwork and signalling is seen to advantage in this view of Slough looking east in about 1905. Slough was the junction for the Windsor branch; this service departed from the bay platform on the right. The line-up of vehicles in the left platform is also of interest: it is apparently being shunted back towards the camera.

The GWR in the landscape. Symonds Yat on the Wye Valley branch is one of countless picturesque locations once served by the railway but now totally devoid of a train service.

Another rural location was Codford between Salisbury and Westbury, although this time the route was a main line. Codford was once the junction for a line to a First World War army camp of the same name, although this had long disappeared by the time the view was taken. Sadly, the station no longer exists either, although at least the line is still open as an important through route linking Bristol with the South Coast. (*J.S. Gilks*)

Another railway absorbed by the GWR from 1923 was the MSWJ system, which had its own station at Savernake almost alongside the GWR station of the same name. Always tightly run financially, the lack of investment may be the reason why the platform is not completely grass-free in this early view, which was certainly unusual for the railways of the period. A large-boilered MSWJ 4-4-0s stands at the head of a northbound train for Swindon and possibly Cheltenham. (*LGRP*)

It is easy to gain the impression that the Great Western was a company of 'Kings' and 'Castles' only, but to do so would be to ignore the myriad byways and rural branches. One of these was the Watlington branch from Princes Risborough and its intermediate stopping place at Lewknor Bridge Halt; the ground-level platform meant steps would have been required. (*LGRP*)

Suburban branch working: a steam commuter service in the form of 57xx 0–6–0PT No. 3697 approaching Bourne End on a service from Paddington in September 1959. The Marlow branch can be seen joining from the right. (*C.R.L. Coles*)

Returning to the main line, this time Bath Spa. The fireman of No. 6814 *Enborne Grange* is adjusting the storm sheet on what is clearly a very wet day. At least there will be less chance of dust from the coal! The train engine is No. 6974 *Bryngwyn Hall* and the locos are working the 8.20 a.m. Bristol (Temple Meads) to Portsmouth Harbour on 17 August 1963. (*B.J. Ashworth*)

Rationalisation in haste! Where the remains of the bracket signal still stand there had once been sidings. The location is Thingley, near to Chippenham, on 19 June 1960, and the train passing is the 5.30 p.m. from Paddington hauled by No. 1002 *County of Berkshire*. (*R.E. James-Robertson*)

Hardly a GWR vehicle in sight – although the third coach does appear to be an all-Third. No. 7015 *Carn Brea Castle* is shown on a Plymouth to Bristol special working, climbing Hemerdon Bank on 6 August 1956. (*T.E. Williams*)

On summer weekends, an often harassed shed foreman would be forced to use almost anything available on passenger and parcels workings. An example is shown here, with 2–8–0 No. 2881 between Dainton and Totnes in August 1956. (*R.J. Blenkinsop*)

Bending vertically over the summit at Dainton, as No. 5918 *Walton Hall* (leading) and No. 1014 *County of Glamorgan* breast the climb with milk tanks in April 1951. (*Michael E. Ware*)

The famous sea-wall at Teignmouth, where passing trains provoke fascination in trippers even today. Unfortunately, No. 6815 *Frilford Grange* is no more, but she survives in this picture in charge of a mid-week excursion to Goodrington Sands in the summer of 1956. (*T.E. Williams*)

More railways and the sea, this time in Dorset, as No. 1369 threads cautiously along the Weymouth Tramway with a train load of passengers from the *Sarnia*. They are bound for Waterloo from the former GWR quay line and station. (*J.C. Haydon*)

At 1250 feet above sea level, the 12.46 p.m. Merthyr to Abergavenny auto-train heads east from Dowlais (High Street) station on 14 August 1957. In the background the Brecon to Newport route can be seen crossing on the bridge. (*S. Rickard*)

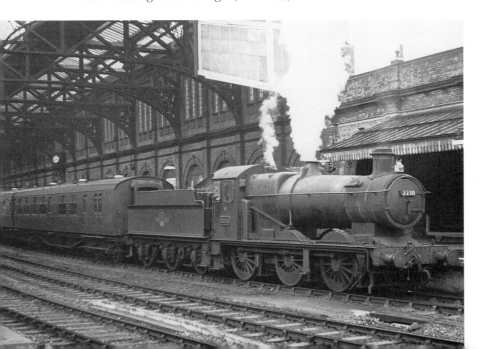

A former Great Western engine but definitely a Southern station and Southern stock. The location is Bournemouth Central, and No. 2230 has charge of the 7.32 p.m. stopping train to Eastleigh in August 1960. (*R.A. Panting*)

Returning west again, with a panoramic view of Gwinear Road station in Cornwall as the Helston branch service departs behind 2–6–2T No. 4500. In later years, passenger traffic from Helston was extremely limited; the branch survived mainly on its broccoli traffic until this too was lost to road competition, and the branch closed in November 1962.

Wrong-line working at Birmingham Snow Hill, with its distinctive signal box visible. The 11.40 a.m. Up service behind No. 6006 *King George I* is being forced to use the Down line as the Up platform was at that time under repair. The date is a very wet 9 October 1960 and the then new BR Mk I coaches appear to make up the whole of the train.

Some years earlier, and No. 6009 *King Charles II* displays the characteristic polished valve spindle covers to the inside cylinders. The engine is in charge of the 3.30 p.m. West of England fast service in Sonning cutting. (*Real Photographs*)

Views of the Hawksworth 'County' class in GW livery are a little uncommon, so this photograph of No. 1011 *County of Chester* at Bristol Temple Meads was something of a pleasurable find. The date is August 1948 and the British Railways era, but it would probably still be some time before the locomotive's GW insignia was replaced. (*H.C. Casserley*)

Almost brand new, the first of the 4–6–0 'County' class, No. 1000 *County of Middlesex*, is in charge of the 5.13 p.m. Weston-super-Mare to Paddington express, made up of the 1935 'Centenary' stock, near Twyford in July 1946. (*M.W. Earley*)

Another 'County' in original condition, as an unidentified member of the class heads a Birkenhead to London train at Halton Tunnel near Chester.

A final view of the class for now, with No. 1022 *County of Northampton* in GWR colours but with 'British Railways' in the GWR lettering style on the tender. The location is Powdenham Park and the train is thought to be the Up mail. A requirement of the GPO was that mail coaches were always marshalled next to the engine. (*Pursey C. Short*)

The 1925 exchange trials between the GWR and LNER saw No. 4079 *Pendennis Castle* running from Kings Cross and showing the prowess of a Swindon machine over the home-grown Doncaster product. The LNER, though, was quick to learn and built some wonderful engines in later years. Sadly, despite the grace of the design, Swindon was content to rest on its laurels and the full potential of the Churchward legacy was probably never developed.

GWR versus LNER at Kings Cross. Although undated the photograph must have been taken during the locomotive trials between the two companies in 1925.

The unhappy experiment in streamlining a GWR 'King', No. 6014 *King Henry VII*, complete with bulbous fittings and recorded by the official photographer. Whether, as rumour has it, these additions came about by the Chief Mechanical Engineer sticking pieces of plasticine onto a model is unclear, although the lack of commitment by the GWR at a time when such adornments were fashionable is readily apparent.

Busy times at Swindon in 1946. No. 5001 *Llandovery Castle*, heading west while an unidentified tender engine reposes at what was then the Down platform.

No. 5090 *Neath Abbey,* a member of the 'Castle' class, seen here coasting over Combe Viaduct into Saltash station on the 12.00 noon Penzance to Manchester and Liverpool service. This was a stopping service as far as Plymouth, after which it was reclassified as the more appropriate express. (*R.E. Vincent*)

A beautifully clean No. 5007 *Rougemont Castle* standing at Bath in June 1954. The engine is coupled to a Hawksworth-style tender and is no doubt running on local duties following overhaul. The wagon turntable in the foreground is also worthy of a second glance. (*W.J. Reynolds*)

What may well be a running-in turn for No. 7017 *G.J. Churchward*, built in August 1948 and therefore an engine that never carried the GWR livery.

No. 6979 *Helperly Hall* waiting for the road at Oxford. Oxford retained semaphore signals until the 1970s; the replacement of these at so many places was yet another sign that the days of Great Western influence had ended.

Departure from Platform 2 at Chester General on 5 June 1963. No. 5098 *Clifford Castle* is displaying the workaday grime that was all too typical of steam in the final years. Next stop Wolverhampton?

The approach to Colwall Tunnel from the west. An early series 43xx 'Mogul' at the head of the 1.40 p.m. Hereford to Worcester service on 5 August 1958. (*P.J. Shoesmith*)

The late George Heiron was renowned equally as a painter and a photographer. His camera shots clearly show his skill and eye for composition. One of his favourite haunts was on the Badminton line, where he captured the Up 'South Wales Pullman' at Westerleigh East in May 1961.

GWR loco and GWR stock. The latest postwar express design, the 10xx 'County' class, represented here by No. 1017 *County of Hereford* at speed.

It is tempting in any photographic miscellany to include just locomotive views, sometimes at the expense of other equally interesting features. In the latter category are some of the services operated, such as this regular mixed passenger/goods working from Stourbridge, recorded here at Platform 12 of Birmingham Snow Hill, with No. 5098 *Upton Castle* in charge. (*B.J. Ashworth*)

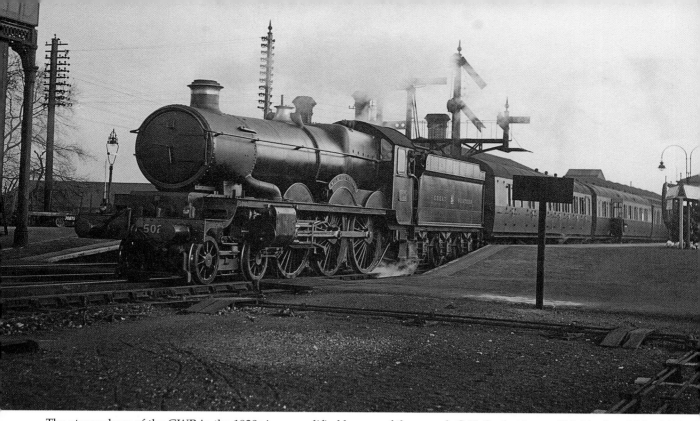

The atmosphere of the GWR in the 1930s is exemplified by one of the superb G.H. Soole views of Maidenhead. No. 5022 *Wigmore Castle* – named after the house near Hereford – is seen ready to depart on an unrecorded working.

Bristol Temple Meads in 1935, viewed from the west – or should it be south? The train is departing south towards Taunton but may be a local working for Weston-super-Mare. Bearing in mind the complexity of the layout the view was clearly taken during a quiet period as only three locomotives are visible. (*Veale & Co.*)

Photographers enjoying a footplate ride on what was probably one of the last 'Dean Goods' in service. Regretfully the location is not recorded.

Freight on the Cardiff–Swansea main line, with 2–8–0T No. 5230 passing under the Pontypridd to Cadoxton branch near St Fagans in June 1949. (*J.C. Flemons*)

Just as it is about to enter Rainbow Hill Tunnel, Worcester, 51xx No. 4162 is shown with the Kidderminster portion of the 'Cathedrals Express' – the 8.34 a.m. from Kidderminster on 30 June 1962. (*Anthony A. Vickers*)

The '517' class of 0–4–2 tank engines entered service from 1868 onwards, with a number surviving until the 1930s. A few stragglers even managed to last until the 1940s, and the very last, No. 1159, is seen here at Blenheim and Woodstock, probably in its final days before being condemned in August 1947. (*Russell Studios*)

For working suburban services around Paddington, Reading and Birmingham, the GWR possessed a large number of 2–6–2Ts, of which No. 5184, built in 1931, was an example. It is seen here about to enter the tunnel at Snow Hill with the 12.20 p.m. stopping service to Leamington Spa. The view was taken in BR days, with the engine in plain black but the background of the numberplate in red. The large girder across the track supported the main wall of the station booking office. (*E.D. Bruton*)

Left: Small 'Prairie' No. 5518 overflowing its tanks at Sharpness on 13 December 1963. (*B.J. Ashworth*)

Below: Majesty at Bristol. No. 6000 *King George V* complete with the bell at Bristol Temple Meads in the early 1930s. (*G.H.*

The GWR's experiment in non-steam main-line traction took the form of two gas-turbine/electric locomotives ordered before nationalisation but in fact delivered some time afterwards. For various reasons neither was totally successful, although the second and larger engine, No. 18100, seen here near Box, was for some time the most powerful engine working on Britain's railways. The gas-turbine is seen here in charge of the Down 'Merchant Venturer' and is about to meet a local goods working consisting principally of ballast wagons. (*G.F. Heiron*)

Night-time at Bristol Temple Meads. The 7.15 p.m. service to Manchester awaits departure from Platform 9 while a pannier tank waits for the signal to clear at Platform 7. (*G.F. Heiron*)

Another evening shot at Bristol, this time with 4–6–0 No. 5076 *Gladiator* at the head of the 6.20 p.m. service to Paddington. (*G.F. Heiron*)

Shrewsbury, August 1961. For a brief moment No. 5059 *Earl St Aldwyn* and No. 5024 *Carew Castle* stand side by side before the latter crosses over and couples up to pilot No. 5059 over the heavy-going stretch of the north-west main line between Shrewsbury and Pontypool Road with a well-loaded 9.05 a.m. from Liverpool to Kingswear and Plymouth. (*Colin Walker*)

Stratford-upon-Avon in the last days of steam. No. 2211 has charge of the 8.43 a.m. local service to Leamington Spa while a diesel multiple unit reposes in the background. (*T.E. Williams*)

Fashions from the mid-1960s. Platform 1 at Weston-super-Mare General in July 1966. (*G.F. Heiron*)

Express services to the west were usually in the hands of the 4-cylinder 'Castle' and 'King' classes, although it was not unknown for one of the slightly smaller 2-cylinder designs to appear. This was the case on 2 August 1952, with an unidentified 'Grange' class 4–6–0 heading west at Fairwood Junction, Westbury, bound for Taunton and Exeter. (*G.J. Jefferson*)

Gloucester Central in the rain. Passengers and staff await the next arrival, while opposite No. 5094 *Tretower Castle* awaits departure with the 7.12 p.m. stopping service to Swindon. (*G.F. Heiron*)

The first of the 'Castle' class to be fitted with double chimneys was No. 7018 *Drysllwyn Castle*, photographed here at Churston Court Farm while undergoing performance analysis at the head of the 'Torbay Express'. The cables from the dynamometer car into the smokebox mar the otherwise neat lines of the engine.

No. 7925 *Westell Hall* accelerating through the site of the old Defiance Platform near Plymouth with the 11.35 p.m. Liverpool to Penzance train on 13 July 1957. (*R.E. Vincent*)

The somewhat unusual combination of a 'Castle' and a 'Dukedog'. No. 7031 *Cromwell's Castle* behind No. 9023 descending Dainton Bank with a Plymouth to Paddington working in March 1954.

No. 5060 *Earl of Berkeley* on the final stretch of the long climb to Savernake Summit with a West of England relief service. To the left is the Crofton pumping station, used to ensure there was sufficient water available in what were the higher reaches of the Kennet and Avon canal.

The other *Earl of Berkeley*, No. 9017, which ran for a while with this name when first built.

On the much lamented cross-country route from Taunton to Barnstaple at Wiveliscombe, No. 7333 is exchanging the single-line token with the signalman. (*R.E. Toop*)

At Dulverton on the Barnstaple line, a junction was formed with services for the Exe Valley route. A 57xx, No. 9685, is seen here leaving the station on an Exe Valley branch line train. (*R.E. Toop*)

Although at first glance similar to the 57xx type, the 54xx and 64xx classes were specifically designed for branch-line workings, being fitted with smaller wheels. Even so, examples of the class would also turn up at main-line sheds from time to time. No. 6422 is seen alongside the coal stage at Wolverhampton Stafford Road in September 1960.

No. 6879 *Overton Grange* passing westwards through Liskeard with a Down freight in May 1959, possibly consisting of empty vans ready for broccoli traffic from Helston. (*M. Mensing*)

A pannier tank, No. 4665, leaving Newbury with the 2.00 p.m. to Lambourn in late September 1959. At this time the branch had but three months left before closure.

Also on the Lambourn line, but this time near to Bockhampton Crossing just south of the terminus, No. 2234 heads a single coach forming the 10.15 a.m. service out of Newbury. With a crew of three and station staff as well, it is perfectly understandable why such services were considered uneconomic. This line closed at the start of January 1960.

Known as a 'Metro Tank', No. 3582 was one of a large class of engines built over a 30-year period from 1869, and used on suburban and branch services throughout the system. Eventually they were ousted by more modern types able to deal better with increasing train weights, although some engines survived into BR ownership; the majority were also recorded as having run in excess of one million miles each. No. 3582 dated from February 1899 and was one of the very last survivors, being in service until November 1949.

The Brecon and Merthyr railway contributed forty-seven locomotives to GWR stock in the grouping 1923, including what became GWR No. 1113, an 0–6–2T built by Robert Stephenson & Co. in April 1914. Originally B & M No. 43 it was renumbered as stated and lasted in service with British Railways until August 1950.

Beautifully clean 4–6–0 No. 5000 *Launceston Castle*, at Old Oak in April 1937. No. 5000 was one of nineteen of the class built in 1926/7 and was also the first of the type to be fitted with a whistle shield from new.

On foreign territory: Nos 2215 and 3604, coupled together for clearance trials over the former Somerset and Dorset line, seen here on Midford Viaduct in December 1958. (*Ivo Peters*)

Another clean engine, 63xx No. 6386, at what may well be Old Oak Common depot. Not always popular with the firemen, the 43xx type and its variants did sterling service on a variety of workings from their introduction in 1911, several of the class surviving until the very end of Western Region steam.

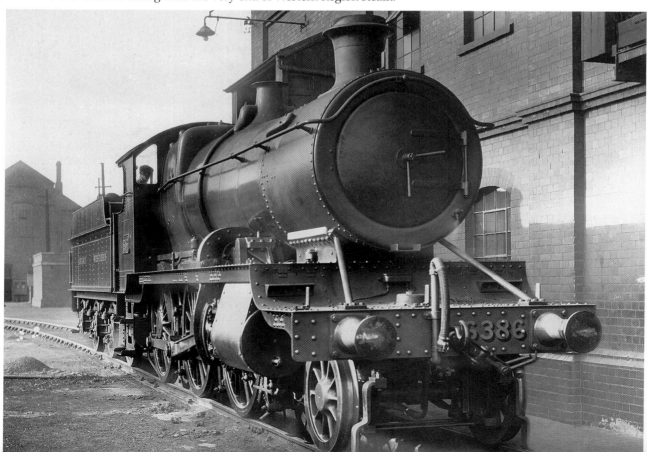

Another railway company absorbed by the GWR in 1923 was the Midland and South Western Junction, which contributed twenty-nine locomotives to stock. One of these, No. 16, was a 2–6–0, one of a pair of almost identical engines. The second engine, No. 14, shown here, was withdrawn from service in 1914 in consequence of a serious crack having been found in its frames. It was subsequently sold, minus its boiler and tender, to Wakes of Darlington in 1918 and rebuilt to work on the Cramlington Colliery line in Northumberland, where it remained in service until 1943.

One of the last survivors of the numerous '850' class of saddle tank engines, No. 1925 was built at Wolverhampton in 1883/4. This and sister engine No. 2007 survived in their original form into the British Railways era and in their final years were allocated to Reading with duties either on the Lambourn branch or shunting the Reading Signal Works yard. Several others of the type survived but were rebuilt with conventional pannier tanks, No. 2012 being the very last of the type to remain in use.

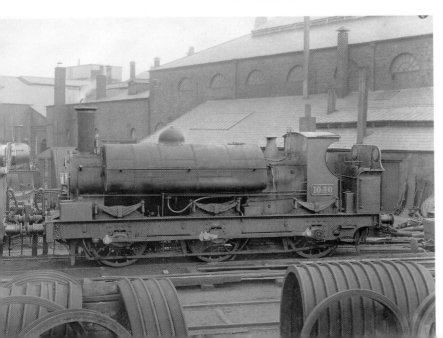

Another elderly 0–6–0T, this time of the Wolverhampton '1016' type, dating from 1870. Originally fitted with wooden brake blocks, cast iron brakes were later fitted. No. 1040 remained in service until January 1929 and was one of the class not to be converted to pannier tanks nor to be superheated.

'Buffalo' class outside-framed 0–6–0T No. 1592 in superb external condition and probably recorded almost as built – note the open water filler atop the tank. The 266 engines in this class were constructed at Swindon and were very much the tank equivalent of the 'Standard Goods' type – albeit with double frames. As with a number of the saddle tank designs, most of the class were later modified with pannier tanks, No. 1592 being so treated in 1911. It remained in service until 1928.

The Cornwall Minerals Railway was amalgamated into the GWR in 1896, having previously been taken over in 1877. Nine engines were involved out of the total stock of eighteen operated by the company and unusually all were of identical type. No. 9 was quickly renumbered 1400 and later given the number 1398 to replace one of the type sold to the Sharpness Dock Co. It is recorded at an unknown location, probably at or near its original haunts sometime prior to December 1912. The point levers are quite wonderful!

Raven, a broad gauge tank engine belonging to the South Devon Railway, which came to the GWR in 1876. It was converted to the standard gauge in 1892, at which time it was renumbered 1329. The location of the photograph is not recorded although it could well be the quayside at Totnes in the locomotive's broad gauge days.

Alan-A-Dale, a former Severn and Wye Railway engine built by Fletcher Jenkins in 1876. Given the number 1355 by the GWR following its takeover of the SWR in 1895 the engine was rebuilt at Swindon in 1896 but remained in service only until 1905.

Former Burry Port and Gwendraeth Valley Railway No. 13 seen here as GWR No. 2165 at Burry Port. Built by Hudswell Clark in 1913, this engine came to the GWR in 1923 and was obviously considered to be a useful machine as it survived in service until March 1955. (*J.N. Westwood*)

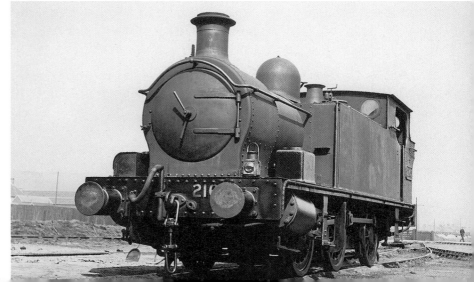

Milk empties from North Acton. No. 9706 leaving North Acton Junction en route to West Ealing Milk Yard on 18 June 1963. (*B.H. Jackson*)

Relegated to menial duties, No. 5057 *Earl Waldergrave* heads a freight train from South Wales to the South of England through Bathampton. Such tasks were often performed by main-line passenger engines considered unsuitable for fast passenger work, often when awaiting overhaul. Another time such scenes were commonplace was in the final years of steam, when diesels were taking over the express workings and steam was being relegated to lesser duties.

Stoneycombe Sidings, Devon. No. 5195 banking a Down goods working up the incline. (*Ernest Rixon*)

Ballast and freight, purportedly near Par, with an unidentified 57xx Pannier in charge.

Abergwilli Junction north of Carmarthen was once the junction of the lines to Aberystwyth and the LMSR linking into the Vale of Towy line. Sadly neither the junction nor either route still survives. In happier times, 57xx No. 7445 comes off the Aberystwyth route heading south with a mixed freight in August 1963. (*Anthony A. Vickers*)

Within the confines of Bristol Docks, No. 8746 finds employment at the head of a rake of cattle wagons sometime in the early 1960s. (*R.E. Toop*)

I could not resist the inclusion of two panniers working hard on what is clearly a heavily graded and severely curved line. Regrettably, neither the location nor date are known, although the photograph does show that the prototype had sharp radius curves as well!

In the days when a daily pick-up goods served each wayside station and ventured out on to the main line between faster services, No. 3739 heads a Down working between Chippenham and Thingley Junction in March 1952. (*G.J. Jefferson*)

Resting at Bathampton. The crew of an unidentified early series 57xx take on water in the loop while waiting to proceed with a short goods bound for Westbury. The train passing westbound at some speed is 2xx No. 2261 on an unknown working. (*Derek Cross*)

A long-forgotten route of the GWR in west London was that to Brentford Dock, where No. 9722 is seen working a permanent way train through a decidedly industrial scene in May 1962. (*L. Sandler*)

Again, I regret, an unknown date and location, and an absolutely filthy locomotive. No. 7800 *Torquay Manor*, an utter disgrace, displays 'Class A' headcode, apparently sometime in the GWR period. (*J.B. Heyman*)

The big 2–8–2T engines of the 72xx class were regular visitors as far south as Salisbury and were ideal for working freight services over the heavily graded route south of Westbury. Here No. 7205 arrives at Salisbury and passes a long line of mixed LSWR and SR vintage stock in the sidings in July 1954.

The lime-washed cattle wagons indicate this is possibly a market special or a train to or from one of the South Wales cattle ports – unfortunately the location is not recorded. The locomotive is a 'Standard Goods' or '388' class 0–6–0 No. 44, built in 1869, which continued in service until 1921.

Reported to have been universally disliked by their crews, the 'Aberdare' 2–6–0 type was very much a slow, plodding goods engine. This one, No. 2620, shows definite evidence of priming and many miles of weary work. The class first appeared in 1900, No. 2620 dating from August 1903. It was photographed on a Down goods near Hayes in 1948, at which time there were only a few of the class remaining. No. 2620 was the penultimate to be withdrawn in August 1949. (*J.D. Cable*)

One of a number of former GWR lines in Devon to have been closed was the Teign Valley branch between Heathfield and Exeter. In the final years only a freight service was operated, as seen here at Trusham behind 4148 in March 1962.

The standard GWR heavy freight design 28xx 2–8–0 No. 3844 passes Dr Day's Junction, Bristol on 3 October 1964 with a Down goods working. (*E. Thomas*)

An Oswestry to Newtown freight leaving Buttington Crossing for Welshpool on 4 August 1956 behind one of the last survivors of the 'Dean Goods' type, No. 2538. (*Geoffrey Bannister*)

The view from Crumlin Viaduct on to the works below in April 1965, with an unidentified 57xx passing the nearby colliery on a typical valleys working. (*P. Hocquard*)

The extensive goods yard at Stoke Gifford on the Badminton line north of Bristol, viewed from the south on a spring morning in 1960. The location still survives, albeit with somewhat reduced siding capacity, and is also the site of the modern-day Bristol Parkway station.

Perishable goods were once an important source for income to the railways from particular growing areas. One of these was west Cornwall around Helston and Penzance. The latter location is seen here, with fresh vegetables being loaded at Ponsandane Sidings.

Manual goods handling. The photograph shows a railway goods shed. Such activity still goes on today, although invariably involving road transport and pallet goods. The location is not confirmed but could well be in the Birmingham area.

Out to grass? Well, almost. Former GWR 15xx pannier tank, No. 1501, sold out of service to the NCB and seen running light to shed at Coventry Colliery in July 1965. (*G.J. Holt*)

Another industrial scene, this time in North Wales, where No. 3709 shunts the sidings at Brymbo Steelworks *circa* 1966. (*Wynn*)

No. 6866 *Morfa Grange*, assisted in the rear by 2–6–2T No. 4100, climbing through the Stroud Valley with the 10.30 a.m. Bordesley Junction to Swindon freight in June 1964. (*B.J. Ashworth*)

Still a favourite among devotees of the GWR, the 'Bulldog' class was used on a variety of workings from cross-country passenger to heavy freight workings. One of the latter is seen here, with No. 3448 *Kingfisher* climbing Hatton Bank with a Down goods. (*H. Weston*)

Compared with the previous view, the crew of No. 4663 have no weight at all behind them and are also keen to work every rest-day as well! Bampton (Devon) station on the Exe Valley route, May 1962. (*D. Holmes*)

Having just passed a Distant signal at caution, the crew of No. 2203, coupled to a small 2500 gallon tender, will no doubt be preparing to stop if required. No location details are known.

With clearance trials over the former Somerset and Dorset route successfully carried out, former GWR No. 3218 is seen working the 1.15 p.m. Evercreech Junction to Highbridge passenger service out of Edington Burtle in February 1965. (*M.J. Fox*)

Cautiously descending the steep bank between Upton Scudamore and Westbury, No. 2898 has charge of a fitted freight, possibly of bananas, from Southampton Docks in the late 1950s.

Local goods working alongside the Dawlish sea-wall: No. 2208 is coupled to a former ROD tender on an Exeter to Newton Abbot working. (*E.D. Bruton*)

Local goods working in Cornwall: Nos. 1664 and 1626 approach the water column on the return trip from Carbean to Goonbarrow Junction with loaded china clay wagons in September 1960.

Proving, if it were ever necessary, that the pannier tank design was the general use engine, No. 1608 heads Down freight on the main line near Teignmouth Quay on 13 July 1959. (*R.C. Riley*)

For many years the workings of the railway at Weymouth Quay went unnoticed by the enthusiast, although fortunately in later years more began to become aware of the fascinating system that existed there. Operations were not confined solely to freight as passenger trains would also slowly wend their way between the traffic, frequently having to stop and wait for an inconsiderately parked vehicle to be moved. No. 1367 is seen here on a Channel Island freight on the quayside in July 1960. (*K.A.V. Hobson*)

A light load for No. 5680 as it passes Pont Cynon Junction on the Aberdare branch in October 1958.

GWR freight in GWR days. An unidentified early series pannier tank – note the open back to the cab – climbing hard on a freight which itself is worthy of a second glance. Sadly, the location is not recorded, although it is almost certainly somewhere in Wales!

Remaining in the Principality, 64xx series 0–6–0T No. 6423 arrives at Nantybwch with the 2.35 p.m. Abergavenny Junction to Merthyr service.

The last of these South Wales studies sees 57xx No. 7724 approaching the Llanbradach Colliery in the Rhymney Valley with an Up working on 27 April 1957.

One of the late Paul Riley's superb studies of working steam. No. 9610 leaves a smoke-screen as it climbs up the grade from Wrexham in March 1966.

A final look at the pannier tank design, with an unidentified 57xx in an unrecorded location shunting a pick-up goods, towards the end of steam. The brake van has been uncoupled and left on the running line and the crew are shunting the siding. The gradient back would no doubt have made for an interesting display from the engine!

They were not all like Box Tunnel, as the charming portal of Tall-y-llyn Tunnel on the Brecon and Dowlais line shows. A modeller's dream – for a fiddle yard!

Fox's Wood Tunnel on the main line near Bristol, in the years prior to 1927. After this time the GWR started the conversion of distant arms of signals to yellow from red, which naturally commenced on the principal routes.

The western end of Box Tunnel in 1959. Most views of this location tend to depict one of the larger 4–6–0 classes on express workings, but it must not be forgotten that such workings played only a very small part in the total number of trains. The photograph shows No. 2265 on a Down goods service. (*J.C. Way*)

Believed to be another of the tunnels on the section between Bath and Bristol, the curvature of the line at this point has resulted in the need to sight the Distant signal on the opposite side of the rails, so that it is visible to the driver in his right-hand position. The fish-tail end of the arm should also be noted.

From tunnels to bridges and inclines: this is the Talybont Incline on the Brecon and Dowlais line.

The GWR near Bodmin in Cornwall at one of the sites where Brunel's famous timber viaducts had been replaced by masonry and steel. (*Aerofilms*)

Subsidence in Wales. This view was taken by a commercial agency to depict a viaduct which required shoring up because of subsidence. Regrettably, further details of the location and date are not given. (*Fox Photos*)

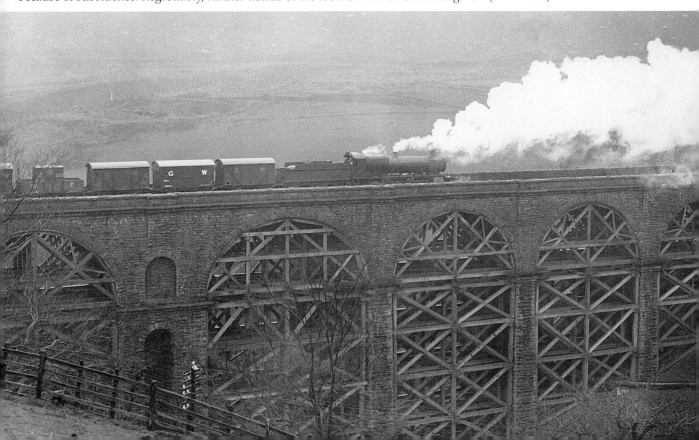

Aynho Junction south of Banbury, and the convergence – or divergence, depending upon one's view – of the Birmingham direct and Oxford lines. The girder bridge took the Down Birmingham direct route over the other lines and so avoided conflicting movements that would otherwise delay traffic.

Flyovers of a different type. The view was taken in connection with the extension of the Ealing and Shepherds Bush Railway and shows Contracts 4 and 5 at Greenford. The large centre span measures 60 feet.

The west end of Newton Abbot station temporarily closed to rail traffic as the former Brunel bridge is demolished to make way for a larger structure. The sleepers across the wagons have caught most of the former roadway, which has just been detonated and will be shovelled by hand into the waiting wagons. (*Mark Wilkins*)

Two stopping trains meet on the Bristol–Avonmouth line by the Portway. The Avonmouth-bound train (approaching) has just left Clifton Down Tunnel, which passes through the cliffs in the background. (*G.F. Heiron*)

No. 4061 *Glastonbury Abbey* approaching Kings Sutton station with a Banbury to Oxford working on the afternoon of 19 April 1952. This engine had been fitted with 'elbow' steam pipes from the outside cylinders in July 1949, and would remain in service until March 1957.

Llanelly shed interior, March 1964.

Permanent way work near Kingsbridge station in 1956. The crew of No. 5551 are able to watch while others work on what was certainly hot work for a summer's day. (*D.A. Bosomworth*)

The interior of the weight house at Swindon Works, recorded in 1980, just a few years before the site would cease to function.

Swindon steam testing in its final years. A Hunslet 'Austerity' 0–6–0T being tested with the Hawksworth dynamometer car after being fitted with various arrangements of blast pipe, chimney and gas-produced systems. The testing programme involving this engine took place at intervals between March and April 1963 and was the last time the Swindon dynamometer car was used with steam.

Left: Embarrassment at Old Oak Common. No details as regards the date or circumstances are reported – but at least it occurred near the depot!

Below: Ready for the belated onset of winter, No. 2227 complete with a temporary snowplough at Gloucester Horton Road in February 1964.

Shown here is 16xx No. 1622, leaving Taplow goods yard with a short freight working which includes the civil engineer's crane.

A short freight working of a different kind, and again hardly economic. Unfortunately it is not quite possible to discern the location from the information on the rear of the print.

A delightful early morning portrait of the 9.05 a.m. passenger service from Minehead leaving the terminus bound for Taunton in August 1955. At this time of day the holidaymakers would be yet to venture outdoors, and yet what a sight they were missing. For the record, 51xx No. 5175 is at the head of the train.

Farewell to the Abbotsbury branch in November 1952. 14xx No. 1454 on one of the last workings over the line, recorded by Stephen Townroe.

Left: Not quite a footplate view, but as close as the layman could get. Token exchange at Westbury (Salop), near Welshpool. The engine is No. 7821 *Ditcheat Manor*, in charge of the 8.05 a.m. Birmingham to Pwllheli service in August 1965.

Below: Another footplate view, this time taken by O.S. Nock from 63xx No. 6316 at Llangollen. The River Dee is on the right.

To add to the photograph included in the first volume of *Odd Corners* is this view of the then new Chipman weedkilling train near Swindon. In charge is an unidentified pannier tank, with the formation including a former 'Toplight' vehicle, now in use as a mess coach, and a much-modified Syphon.

A brief look now at the variety of rolling stock, both goods and passenger, that could be seen on the GWR. To start with, a bogie iron mink. These were far less common than their 4-wheeled counterparts and as can be seen, this example was branded to work on a particular route only. It has also been vacuum fitted, while the oval buffers allowed for shunting around tight curves and reduced the chance of buffer-lock.

The only known view of a 16 ft 6 in iron mink – the majority were 6 in shorter. No. 1607 was recorded at the time of its construction in June 1888 and with a wonderful array of early stock just visible in the background.

In the days before refrigeration, fish was packed in ice and transported in either open or closed vehicles to reach the market as quickly as possible. The importance of moving fish traffic at speed from port to market led the GWR to modify as well as build some strange-looking bogie brake vans, basically an open wagon with a guard's compartment pitched at the mid-point. They were supplemented by this unique 6–wheeled version, No. 42800, which was originally liveried in grey but later changed to brown at the time of renumbering.

A number of the railway companies had glass-lined milk tanks, the six wheels being necessary to reduce lateral movement when running at speed and lessen the chances of the contents arriving as butter! The vehicles were glass-lined for ease of cleaning and sported a bright red livery offset by gold lettering.

Another mink van, No. 96881, and probably just outshopped judging by the livery.

Largest of all the goods wagons on the GWR was the solitary Crocodile L. Built to carry a single load of up to 120 tons, it had two interchangeable bodies so that the load could be underslung – as would be the case here – or carried on top of a conventional low girder arrangement. It was introduced in 1929 and was available for use in either form by 1930.

The standard open wagon of the 1930s, a 5-plank vehicle, with the side door sloped slightly so as to ease the use of sack trucks. The 'Not Common User' branding is a little unusual as this identification was normally applied to those vehicles of this type that were vacuum braked.

One of several similar, but not identical, inspection saloons built for the use of the respective Divisional Civil Engineering Departments from about 1894 onwards. The outside veranda afforded the opportunity to view the track ahead while being propelled, while on some of the saloons a seat, albeit with seat belts, was bolted onto the buffer beam to allow an even closer look!

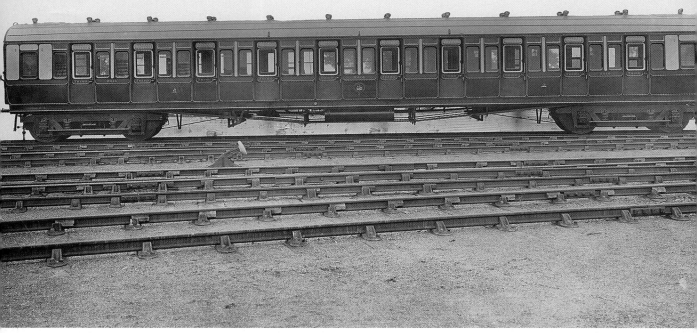

The 70 ft coach designs owed their origins to the incumbency of George Jackson Churchward. One of this type was the 'Toplight', also produced in a shorter 57 ft version. Seen here is an all-Third built in September 1909, complete with the garter crest of the period.

Unlike the LNER, the Great Western's venture into articulation for coaches was limited. On the suburban train sets, a total of 15 vehicles was involved, comprising a mixture of three coaches, a Brake Third, Full Third and First/Third Composite. The connection between two of the vehicles shown here survived in this form from 1925 until withdrawn in the late 1950s.

The other use of articulation was on main-line working, with a kitchen car sandwiched between two dining saloons. All were short vehicles, the kitchen vehicle being the longest at just 47 ft. The formation remained intact until probably the late 1930s, when the vehicles were separated and rebuilt on conventional bogies.

A 70 ft restaurant car of 1913 built to Diagram H22. The livery is the crimson lake of the period, with longitudinal gas cylinders to supply fuel for cooking. The coach's weight meant that it was carried on two 6-wheeled bogies.

A study of ends, beginning with what is believed to be a clerestory slip coach from the turn of the twentieth century but unusually with the guard's side lookouts not visible. The method of working at the time was for the guard to lower the central window and turn off the steam heat and vacuum cocks by hand; the actual practility of this must be open to some question.

End view of a 'Concertina' slip, which measured no less than 9 ft over its maximum width. Fifteen of this type were built in 1906, the last still operating in its original guise on the Bicester slip in 1959.

In this view of a 'Toplight' slip from the 1910–23 period, the panelled ends of the period are shown to advantage, as are the stays intended as additional security to prevent the vehicle body moving longitudinally on the frames. Notice also the guard's handbrake lever visible in the centre window.

One of only three 60 ft double-ended slip coaches of Diagram F23 and built in 1929. All survived into BR ownership but were later altered with the left-hand end window reduced in size.

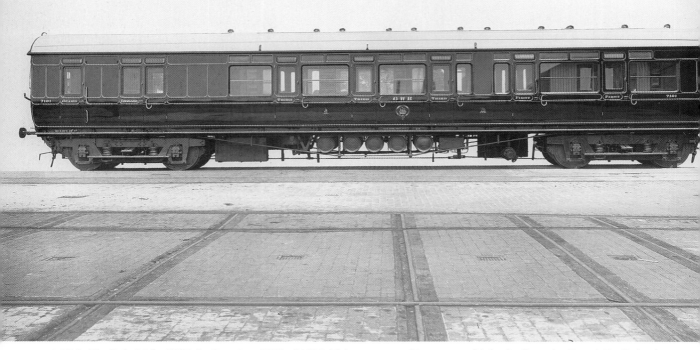

A 57 ft 'Toplight', No. 7101, built to Lot 1150 of 1908. This was one of just two vehicles built to the Bars 1 Toplight design under this lot number and is shown here when brand new from Swindon. The number of additional vacuum reservoirs on the underframe should be noted.

A 70 ft 'Toplight' slip of similar design to the previous coach, this time dating from 1916. Officially, crimson lake livery was still in use at this time, although it would not be long before a change was made to a wartime all-over brown.

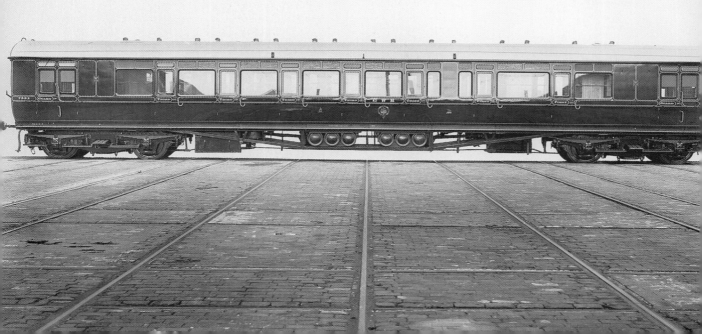

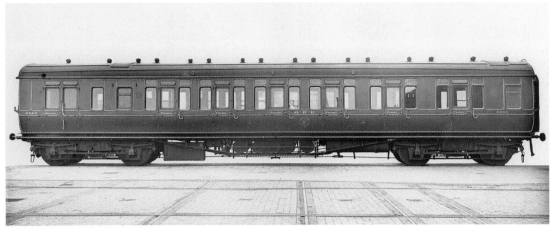

A 'Toplight' slip conversion. No. 6963 started life as a standard 70 ft Brake Composite, but was converted to a single-ended slip coach in the 1920s.

Composite slip No. 7071 of 1938, one of six vehicles built at this time. The fact that there is a guard's compartment at either end indicates this was a double-ended slip coach, the principles of design and operating the system changing little from 1869 to the last working in 1960.

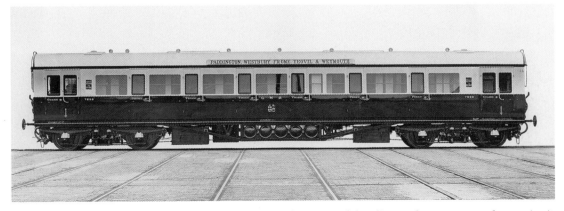

No. 7898 complete with informative roofboard. The advantage of the slip coach system was the service it afforded lesser stations without the need for the train to stop, although this could not apply to collecting intending passengers. At the peak of this operating system some trains would have up to four slip portions, each under the control of a separate guard, and often comprising two or even three vehicles.

Above: Starting a brief look at signalling – or perhaps it would be more appropriate to state Train Control – with a view of Maidenhead in late December 1946. The driver of an unidentified and somewhat grimy 51xx/61xx tank engine collects the token for the first stage of a journey along the line to High Wycombe, which will take in Bourne End, Wooburn Green and Loudwater en route.

Left: Actual signal replacement work on the ground appears to have been rarely recorded, although here a former GWR wooden post signal is in the process of being changed to the new metal post alongside. The location is the Up line of the Uxbridge branch at West Drayton and although the date is not recorded it may well be during the early 1950s. (*G.J. Jefferson*)

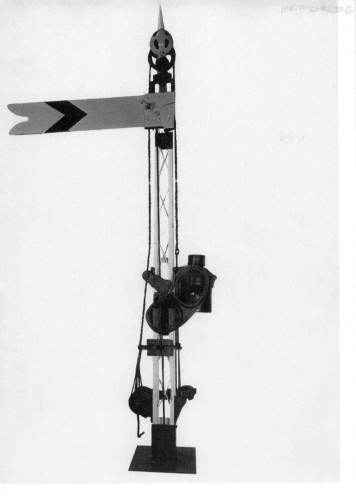

Above left: A full-size model of a post-1927 painted Distant signal with a windlass attached. In this way the complete spectacle arm and lamp could be lowered to ground level for cleaning and servicing, thereby avoiding the need for the lampman to climb the post.

Above right: An early example of a motor-operated Distant signal, at the time clearly still painted red.

Left: What was probably one of the last fishtail-ended Distant signals recorded still in use probably in the late 1950s. The fishtail end was seen as preferable to the conventional cut end as it lessened the risk of the wooden arm splitting along its length, although the use of small ties across the rear and later metal arms resolved any such difficulties.

Signals in the landscape at Morfa Mawddach near Barmouth in 1966, with No. 75030 on the northbound daily freight passing the remains of a bracket signal and a rather nice shunting arm complete with 'cash register'.

Athelney signal-box on the route from Castle Cary to Taunton, with an 0–4–0 Fowler-built contractors diesel en route from its work in assisting the lifting of track on the former Devizes branch to similar work on the Barnstaple branch from Taunton in July 1967. (*John C. Sawtell*)

Largest of all the mechanical signal-boxes on the former GWR was Reading West Main, where three men together with what is probably a lineman can be seen. Although clearly posed, the view is little different from real life, the signal-man studying the diagram to indicate the progress of the train before confirming its passage with a glance for the tail lamp.

Mechanical signalling development in the 1940s. The left view shows the interior of the signal-box with the electrically-operated point lever in the reverse position. Notice the short handle and also the hand generator for the points in the background. In the centre is the apparatus case for the batteries used for the detection and finally on the right the signal controlling entry to the loop points at the remote location. Such electrical equipment was installed at a number of sites on the GWR during the 1940s and enabled points and crossings to be controlled from considerably greater distances than with conventional mechanical means. Although the location is not specified, the finials on the signals are of the type used by Westinghouse during work on the North and West line around Wooferton at this period.

Mechanical signalling in its last hours. Woodborough signal box at 1.30 a.m. on 22 January 1979, just before it closed for the final time.

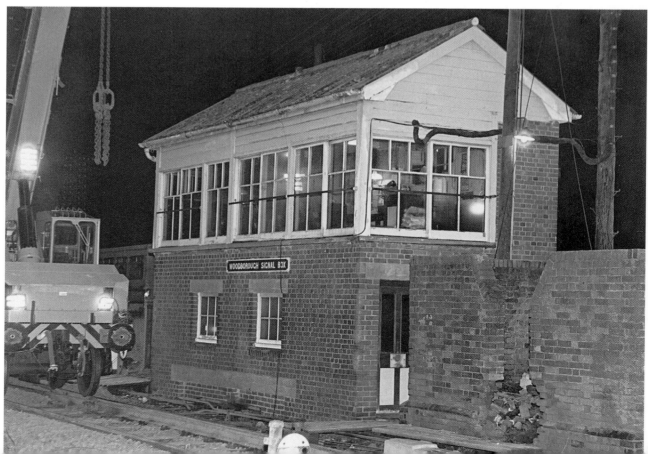

Left: Signalman Jim Hughes displays a caution flag to an approaching service – the reason for which is not reported – from his box at Scours Lane near Reading. Notice the former windows of the locking room have been bricked in; no doubt a wartime precaution that was never altered. (*Cecil J. Blay*)

Below: Ufton Crossing signal-box with signalman R. F. (Bob) East in charge. (*D. Canning*)

Non-illuminated track diagram from Thatcham station near Newbury. As was standard practice, all the point connections were 'trailing', while the slotting arrangements for the Up Distant signals throughout should also be noted. This was due to the close proximity of the next box eastwards at Colthrop Crossing.

The GWR in an isolated rural location, at Princetown, high on Dartmoor, in April 1954. In charge of what is reported to be a special train for the Caravan Club is 44xx No. 4410.

On the varying levels between the Severn Tunnel and Patchway, an unidentified 42xx/52xx has charge of a heavy eastbound coal train sometime in the 1930s. (*G.H. Soole*)

'Duke' class 4–4–0 No. 3275 *St Erth*, possibly somewhere in Cornwall and photographed before bulk road track had been abolished.

A view that has been recorded before but its interest factor certainly warrants further inclusion. Presumably the right-hand engine is or has been assisting, as the train certainly appears fully laden. Other circumstances are not known, although it may well be that the location is in the Whitehall. area

The short-lived 'South Wales Pullman' service at rest at Swansea after arrival from Paddington in December 1955. (J.N. Westwood)

The now completely obliterated station at Witham, west of Frome, on the former Weymouth line. Pannier tank No. 3773 is in charge of a train for the Cheddar Valley route through to Wells in the days before part of the branch was given over to aggregate traffic from Merehead. (*R.E. Toop*)

Sights – and sounds – such as this at Wiveliscombe on the Barnstaple line from Taunton are now just a memory. No. 7326 calls with the 11.45 a.m. all-stations service from Taunton in the days before Dr Beeching.

Ballingham Halt on the Hereford to Gloucester route in the final days before its closure in 1959. No. 4161 pauses briefly with the 1.55 p.m. Gloucester-bound service.

Bath Road-based 'Castle', No. 5052 *Earl of Radnor* at Bristol Temple Meads on a dark December evening in 1960. The presence of the LMS coach behind the tender indicates this may possibly have been a Gloucester working. (*J.R. Smith*)

The Moretonhampstead line was one of numerous such dead-end branches serving small settlements off the main lines. Here traffic rarely warranted more than an engine and a single coach. No. 1427, formerly No. 4827, at the terminus ready to return to Newton Abbot.

A cross-country route that is also no longer operational ran through the Cotswolds, including the station at Bourton-on-the-Water. No. 5173 takes a passenger working past the goods shed, which seems to have little traffic.

No. 4663 leaving Chard (Central) for Chard Junction on the main line between Salisbury and Exeter and about to pass a Southern-design rail-built stop signal. The date is Friday 7 September 1962 and the train the 5.30 p.m. service. The signal was apparently faulty that day and the signalman had given permission for the train to proceed past the signal at danger. (R.G. Turner)

Milk on the Hemyock branch from Tiverton Junction, where the operation of milk tanker trains outlived steam, continuing well into the 1970s. The train has paused at the hand-operated level crossing at Cold Harbour Halt, and a member of the crew is in the process of opening the gates.

The Hemyock branch service, with a single coach hauled by a 14xx.

Another Devon branch line, this time from Launceston to Plymouth. No. 5544 calls at Lydford, midway along the line, with the 12.40 p.m. Plymouth service in August 1962. (*L. Sandler*)

A branch line in Wales. Llwycoed looking towards Merthyr in September 1962.

A branch line in the Midlands. Market Drayton station on 4 August 1959. No. 4120 is about to depart with the 12.52 from Crewe to Wellington. (*P.J. Shoesmith*)

The GWR in the 1930s. The location is the busy junction at Westbury and the convergence of the routes to and from the West of England, Bristol and Salisbury. One of the early batch of 'Saint' class 4–6–0s, No. 2902 *Lady of the Lake* leaves with a local service, possibly to Taunton, and passes some rather magnificent signals. This engine was built in 1906 and survived into public ownership, being withdrawn in 1949.

A superbly clean 'Hall' class 4–6–0, No. 6937 *Conyngham Hall*, on what may well be a running-in turn at Didcot on a local freight working from Moreton Yard in November 1963.

The South Wales direct or Badminton line has always been susceptible to flooding, especially in the area of Chipping Sodbury. An example of this was in November 1954 when No. 7020 *Gloucester Castle* had to pick its way out of floodwater that in places was 2 ft 6 in deep. (*Phipps*)

The Greenford to Ealing Broadway auto-train at West Ealing in May 1952. In charge is 54xx No. 5410.

The auto-train of the 1930s. A '517' class 0–4–2T, the forerunner to the 48xx (14xx) class, at Newton Abbot in 1934. Regrettably the working on which No. 1487 was employed is not recorded.

Local working in west Wales. No. 5713 leaving the tunnel near to Wolf's Castle Halt with the 2.10 p.m. Fishguard Harbour to Clarbeston Road service in June 1958.

57xx No. 3646 at an unknown station. The engine was allocated to Banbury in the 1950s, when this photograph was taken, so it is possible it could be in the Oxfordshire area.

No. 4647 taking water at Bristol Temple Meads before departing with the 1.30 (Saturday only) all-stations to Frome via Radstock. The date was 31 October 1959, the last day of passenger working over the line.

The 4.10 p.m. Brecon to Hereford branch service proceeding over the Wye bridge at Whitney on 28 May 1962.

Yatton station south of Bristol. No. 1415 is probably on a Cheddar Valley working complete with 'B' set soon after nationalisation.

Another 14xx complete with BR smokebox numberplate but still displaying GWR livery on an auto-working.

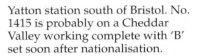

In the days when the Western Region had taken over operation of some of the former Southern Railway branch lines in Devon, No. 1450 leaves Seaton on an auto-working for Seaton Junction in February 1965. (*W.L. Underhay*)

Hatch Tunnel on the Taunton to Chard branch. No. 3736 emerges into the daylight with the 8.00 a.m. from Taunton on 31 August 1962. Notice the width of the tunnel, which had been built originally to accommodate a double track. (*R.G. Turner*)

Pershore station in Worcestershire. The engine still has its original number of 4813 – later to become 1413. The trailer is one of the original matchboard-type vehicles and is being used on what was a conventional auto-working.

A Saltash to Plymouth North Road service at Devonport in August 1949. No. 6421 pauses briefly on what was in effect a local commuter service for the area.

The area where the GWR auto and rail-motor services had their origins – the Stroud Valley. No. 8743 at Stonehouse on the 4.40 p.m. Gloucester to Chalford service in June 1962.

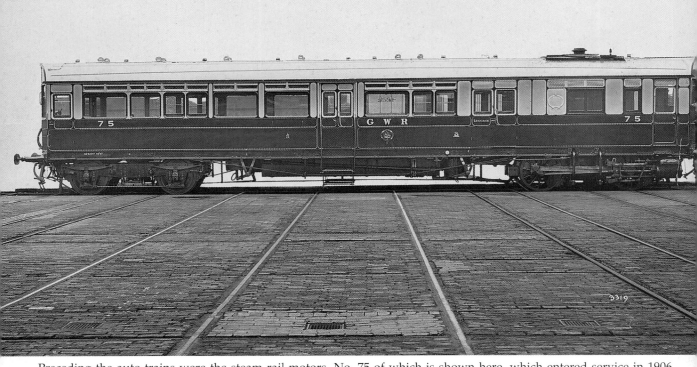

Preceding the auto-trains were the steam rail-motors, No. 75 of which is shown here, which entered service in 1906. Used on a variety of services throughout the system, the design was nevertheless considered obsolete by the 1930s. The Great Western Society hopes to restore a vehicle of similar type within the next few years.

One of the earlier matchboard-type rail-motors and an unknown location – the board on the rear of the engine alongside refers to 'Aldgate'! Servicing rail-motors was a major problem: although they were principally a coach, they had to be worked on in a locomotive shed environment.

On the Portishead branch. A three-car GWR-design diesel unit approaching Clifton Bridge station from Portishead in July 1953. (*C.R.L. Coles*)

Single-car unit No. 20 pauses at Wyre Forest station with the 4.10 p.m. Kidderminster to Tenbury service in June 1959. (*M. Mensing*)

Attracting an admiring glance from the ladies on the opposite platform, one of the original 'streamlined' design single-vehicle railcars being loaded with churns, probably not long after its introduction in 1934.

Under Western Region control the prefix 'W' was added to the numbers of the diesel railcars. No. W48 approaches Wells City station with the 3.36 p.m. arrival (3.49 p.m. departure) to Witham on 22 June 1954. (*E.W. Field*)

A final view of a branch-line train, although in an urban setting. No 1426 at the head of the Staines–West Drayton auto in the summer of 1952.

Steam at work. No. 6950 *Kingsthorpe Hall* heading three 28xx class 2–8–0s and a WD 2–8–0 past Swindon in April 1955. All the engines appear to be in steam. In later years, such sights were commonplace as engines destined for the scrap yards were hauled on their last journeys.

The Mutual Improvement Class at Swindon in 1907 in front of No. 2903 *Lady of Lyon*. Such classes existed throughout the GWR and other railway companies, the staff willingly giving up their free time in an effort to improve their knowledge at work.

Steam in its final days. Croes Newydd shed at Wrexham in 1965. (*Bowman*)

The long progression from starting on the railway to becoming a driver began with cleaning. Two young lads apply elbow grease to No. 6008 *King James II*, possibly at Old Oak Common.

The steam shed outside and within. The depot is unknown but even so the lack of roofing should be noted. Such poor conditions were all too common in the last years of steam. The engine is No. 7812 *Erlestoke Manor*, now preserved on the Severn Valley Railway.

St Philip's Marsh shed, Bristol in 1962 – code 82B. No. 7020 *Gloucester Castle* is a visitor from the neighbouring Bristol Bath Road depot. (*Philip Kelley*)

The locomotive exchanges of 1948. No. 3802 has just completed a Bristol to Eastleigh freight working and the remaining coal is being weighed off at Eastleigh shed in order to provide information on consumption.

Aberystwyth shed in July 1934. Ex-Cambrian 0–6–0 No. 895 is under the shear legs and possibly having attention to its axleboxes. (*J.S. Hancock*)

Cardiff Canton depot in BR days, with predominance of freight engines. Locomotives would be prepared outside regardless of the weather. There must be doubts about the stability of the load of coal on the tender of No. 2867. (*G.F. Heiron*)

Worcester Works in the last days of steam, with Nos. 6821, 6871 and 7318 all receiving attention for what was undoubtedly the final time. (*J.R. Hunt*)

This notice from the Swindon Works is self-explanatory!

SWINDON WORKS HOOTER				
	MONDAY to THURSDAY		FRIDAY	
	TIME	DURATION	TIME	DURATION
MORNING	6·45	17 SECS	6·45	17 SECS
	7·20	12 SECS	7·20	12 SECS
	7·25	7 SECS	7·25	7 SECS
	7·30	12 SECS	7·30	12 SECS
	12·30	12 SECS	1·30	12 SECS
AFTERNOON	1·05	12 SECS		
	1·10	7 SECS		
	1·15	12 SECS		
	4·30	12 SECS		

Discharging ash at Old Oak Common.

Worcester Works in the summer of 1959, with former Ivatt class 4 2–6–0 No. 43017 under repair. (*N. Caplan*)

The first of the two gas turbine/electric locomotives operated by the Western Region, though they had originally been ordered by the GWR. No. 18000 is seen at Corsham near Chippenham on a Bristol to Paddington service, a route on which it was a regular performer. (*G.J. Jefferson*)

Transition from steam, No. 4938 *Liddington Hall* passes D600 *Active* near Bath Spa in July 1960. The variety of vintage internal combustion vehicles in the foreground is arguably just as interesting.

Three varieties of Western Region diesel lurk in the background at Bristol Temple Meads as No. 1013 *County of Dorset* waits to set off with the 6.50 p.m. Weston-super-Mare to Swindon service in July 1964.

Opposite: Bristol, with BR Standard design 'Britannia' class engine No. 70022 *Tornado*. The non-WR design is attracting a lot of attention from the spotters.

November 1964, and the remains of No. 5054 *Earl of Ducie* in 'C' shop at Swindon.

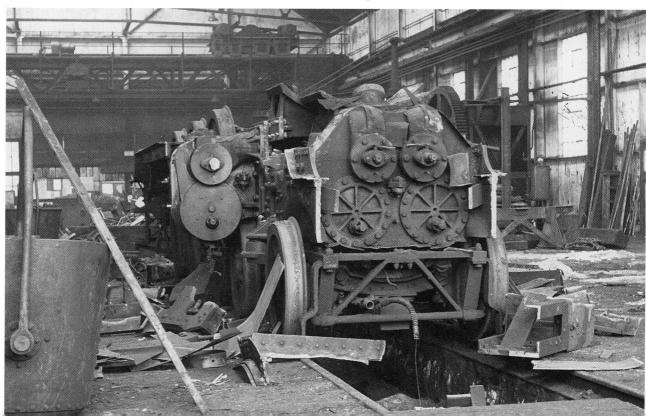

The new order – diesel superpower near Bath
in October 1965. (*G.F. Heiron*)

Clean diesels, whose designs are themselves now faded memories. 'Hymek' No. D7024 and 'Warship' No. D848 *Sultan* outside Swindon Works.

The driver's-eye view. Birmingham Snow Hill as seen on approaching from Moor Street in GWR days.

CAFE

1369

DANGER
KEEP 50 FT CLEAR